They who dance
Find infinite golden floors
Beneath their feet.

Marjorie Allen Seiffert

Other books in the *"Language of"* Series...

Blue Mountain Arts®

It's Great to Have a Brother like You

It's Great to Have a Sister like You

The Language of Brides

The Language of Courage and Inner Strength

The Language of Friendship

The Language of Happiness

The Language of Love

The Language of Marriage

The Language of Parenting

The Language of Positive Thinking

The Language of Prayer

The Language of Recovery

The Language of Success

The Language of Teaching

The Language of Teenagers

Thoughts to Share with a Wonderful Daughter

Thoughts to Share with a Wonderful Father

Thoughts to Share with a Wonderful Mother

Thoughts to Share with a Wonderful Son

Words of Comfort ...for You in Your Time of Loss

You Will Always Have an Angel Watching Over You

The Language of
DANCE

A Blue Mountain Arts® Collection
to Celebrate the Magic of Dance

Blue Mountain Press™

SPS Studios, Inc., Boulder, Colorado

The publisher wishes to acknowledge and thank Gwendolyn Kolupke Gray for her work in compiling and editing the poems and quotations in this collection, as well as the SPS Studios creative staff.

Library of Congress Catalog Card Number: 2001005881
ISBN: 0-88396-624-7

ACKNOWLEDGMENTS appear on page 48.

Certain trademarks are used under license.

Manufactured in Thailand
First Printing: January 2002

 This book is printed on recycled paper.

Library of Congress Cataloging-in-Publication Data

The language of dance : a Blue Mountain Arts collection.
      p. cm. — (The "Language of" Series...)
   ISBN: 0-88396-624-7 (hardcover : alk. paper)
1. Dance—Quotations, maxims, etc. I. SPS Studios. II. Series.
PN6084.D34 L36   2002
792.8—dc21

2001005881
CIP

SPS Studios, Inc.
P.O. Box 4549, Boulder, Colorado 80306

Contents

(Authors listed in order of first appearance)

To Dance

I want to dance!
When the sun catches the aspen leaves
They dance;
When it flecks the grasses and mottles the streams
They dance;
When the dark storm bends the black branches
And the wind whips up the waves
They dance;
The bird swings on the elm twig,
The sap races in the tree,
Horses run in the pasture,
Mist fairies glide to and fro in the valley,
Cloud children play in heaven,
The stars sing and dance,
And I want to dance!
I can be raindrops.
I can be leaves and bending grasses,
Gold-mottled streams and running horses,
Racing sap and the hidden heart of flowers.
I can be firelight and moonlight,
A child of the night mist and a sister of the stars.
All the world sings and dances,
And I am a child of all the world. I want to sing, and —
I want to dance.

Margaret B. McGee

The world of dance is a charmed place.
Some people like to inhabit it, others
to behold it; either way it is rewarding.

— Margot Fonteyn

The dance is one of many human experiences which cannot
be suppressed. Dancing has existed at all times, and among
all people and races. The dance is a form of expression given
to man just as speech, philosophy, painting or music.

— Mary Wigman

I feel that the essence of dance is the expression of man —
the landscape of his soul.

— Martha Graham

How can I describe the joy of dancing?... Voluminous, vast, swelling like sails in the wind, the movements of my dance carry me onward — onward and upward, and I feel the presence of a mighty power within me which listens to the music and then reaches out through all my body, trying to find an outlet for this listening.

☆ Isadora Duncan

To leap becomes, while it lasts,
heart pounding, breath hurting,
the deepest, the only joy.

☆ Denise Levertov

There's a reward in dancing that's indescribable....
the mental and physical coming together. And
when everything is right... there's no other
feeling like it and you remember that and
you'll do almost anything to feel that again.

☆ Robert Weiss

They Who Dance

The feet of dancers
Shine with laughter,
Their hearts are vibrant as bells;

The air flows by them
Divided, like water
Before a gleaming ship.

Triumphantly their bodies sing,
Their eyes
Are blind with music.

They move through threatening ghosts,
Feeling them as cool as mist
Against their brows.

They who dance
Find infinite golden floors
Beneath their feet.

Marjorie Allen Seiffert

Dancing derives its source from pleasure and gaiety of heart, for instinct teaches us, as in all the animal creation, when we are delighted, to express our *allégresse* by laughing, singing, and by different motions of the body and its members: our features become animated, our eyes more brilliant — they express our inward feelings, and joy lifts us... off the ground.

E. A. Théleur

For the good are always the merry,
Save by an evil chance,
And the merry love the fiddle,
And the merry love to dance.

William Butler Yeats

I shall sing a song of joy
With my hair flying;
The wind shall be my loved one....

I shall dance, I shall sing;
I shall sing a song of joy
Up to the stars.

Annette Wynne

When I leap,
I briefly see the world as it is
And as it should be.

Cornelius Eady

Dance, my heart! Dance today with joy.

The streams of love fill the days and nights with music,
and the world is listening to its melodies.

Mad with joy, life and death dance to the rhythm of
this music. The hills and the sea and the earth dance.
The world of man dances in laughter and tears.

Songs of Kabir

To Dance Is to Be Free

I dance, because dancing has always been my salvation... the ultimate freedom!

Ghislaine Thesmar

With a motion of complete joy, as a free being in a world of infinite depth and beauty, I surrender myself to the unseen pulsation of the Universe.

Ruth St. Denis

Dance, when you're broken open.
Dance, if you've torn the bandage off.
Dance in the middle of the fighting.
Dance in your blood.
Dance, when you're perfectly free.

Jalal Al-Din Rumi

On with the dance! Let joy be unconfined.

George Gordon, Lord Byron

The human body should... express all the sensations
or emotions that it experiences. The human body
is ready to express, and it would express if it
were at liberty to do so, all sensations just as
the body of an animal.

Loie Fuller

The aesthetics of dance — the beauty of it, the line
of it, the physicality of it — that's communication...
that's freedom!

Arthur Mitchell

Beauty in Motion

The music's sound, the rhythmic dance,
The happy faces flushed, the feet
Time keeping to the music's beat,
The lovely limbs, the tender glance!

O what more beautiful than this?

Arthur Peterson

I watch the dancer,
Bending,
Lithely stooping,
Leaping, rippling,
Her motions changing
As though she were a song of many notes;
Her white robes swaying,
Her scarves like water under wind;
Her face held up to joy
As a leaf to sunlight;
Her arms yearning and crying out for beauty,
Reaching up
And pulling down beauty upon her head,
Then flinging it from her, to our outstretched hands.

Mary Carolyn Davies

Dancing expresses in a different language,
different from nature, the beauty of the body;
and the body grows more beautiful with dancing.

☆ Isadora Duncan

When you dance it seems to me
As if, in a tall wood
A thousand birds of dawn
Awake to greet the day
Outdoing one another there
With lovely things to say.

☆ Anonymous

When you do dance, I wish you
A wave o' the sea, that you might ever do
Nothing but that.

☆ William Shakespeare

Love's True Expression

Dancing is as old as love.

Lucian

Our love is like slow dancing, and each time we dance, we dance better. We know each other's next move. We feel the music in our bodies, and we move to its rhythm.

Larry D. Tyler

O, Love's but a dance,
    Where Time plays the fiddle!
See the couples advance —
O, Love's but a dance!
A whisper, a glance —
    "Shall we twirl down the middle?"
O, Love's but a dance,
    Where Time plays the fiddle!

Austin Dobson

This wondrous miracle did Love devise,
For dancing is love's proper exercise.

Sir John Davies

The essence of the art of dancing lies in the realm of the soul and heart; it is not the intellect but the emotions from which the dance takes off.

Erika Hanka

When dance achieves its true purpose, it cannot help but touch the hearts of its participants — whether they are sitting motionless in the audience or leaping valiantly through the air onstage.

Dana Landry

A dancer is devoted to, and often consumed by, a love for his or her art like no other artist is. Thus, works of dance become creations of unparalleled love... and so fulfilling to experience.

Jane Andrews

Human beings are born with the instinct to express themselves through movement. Even before he could communicate with words, primitive man was dancing to the beat of his own heart.

Robert La Fosse

Born to Dance

From the moment you could first move
you wriggled and
waggled your way around
inside your mother's womb
you circled around
and around again
trembling forward
then backward
picking up the tempo
with wings on your little feet
you swung wide
first this way then
back the other way
always buzzing
quivering with anticipation of
bursting out ready
to busy yourself on
the dance floor of life.

Charles Portolano

All of my life is a dance.
When I was young and feeling the earth
My steps were quick and easy.
The beat of the earth was so loud
That my drum was silent beside it.
All of my life rolled out from my feet
Like my land which had no end as far as I could see.
The rhythm of my life was pure and free.
As I grew older my feet kept dancing so hard
That I wore a spot in the earth
At the same time I made a hole in the sky.
I danced to the sun and the rain
And the moon lifted me up
So that I could dance to the stars.
My head touched the clouds sometimes
And my feet danced deep in the earth
So that I became the music I danced to everywhere.
It was the music of life.
Now my steps are slow and hard
And my body fails my spirit.
Yet my dance is still within me and
My song is the air I breathe.
My song insists that I keep dancing forever.
My song insists that I keep rhythm
With all of the earth and the sky.
My song insists that I will never die.

☆ Nancy Wood

✳ Dance Is Life ✳

I think the reason dance has held such an ageless magic for the world is that it has been the symbol of the performance of living.... Many times I hear the phrase "the dance of life." It is an expression that touches me deeply, for the instrument through which the dance speaks is also the instrument through which life is lived — the human body. It is the instrument by which all the primaries of life are made manifest. It holds in its memory all matters of life and death and love.

※ Martha Graham

The call to dance is a response to a primitive urge to rhythmic motion. It is an unavoidable internal rhythm of life.

※ Dorothy Buck

The dancer moves; she changes. Aware of her relationship to time and space, she moves through all dimensions, giving context and meaning to life. The dancer is the personification of our natural rhythm and creativity; she is the spark of creation itself.

※ Diane Mariechild

Dancing is the loftiest, the most moving, the most beautiful of the arts, because it is no mere translation or abstraction from life; it is life itself.

— Havelock Ellis

The dance is an art derived from life itself, since it is nothing more nor less than the action of the whole human body; but an action transposed into a world, into a kind of space-time, which is no longer quite the same as that of everyday life.

— Paul Valéry

Movement is the essence of life, dance its ultimate expression.... Life only lasts the very moment of our awareness of it, and all that remains is, as in the dance, the memory we can retain of it.

— Walter Sorell

Dancing is like life. The lessons of one are the lessons of the other.

— Savion Glover

The Universe Is Dancing

The rhythm of the universe, like the rhythm of
our pulses, determines the rhythm of the dance.

☆ Helen Plotz

One only need spend an afternoon observing the scene on a
busy street to know that all of life is a dance: shoppers side-stepping
through crowds; drivers weaving past one another; lovers grasping and
leading each other; and children hopping, sliding, skipping, sulking,
and leaping through the world.

☆ Jane Andrews

Suddenly I see a paper flying in the air. It is floating with
graceful majesty, without a single repetition in its movements, down
along the walls of this gigantic masonry.

The paper, on wings of illusion, [is] performing an unheard-of
dance: yielding to gravity, catching its balance at the right moment,
and again challenging its imaginary equilibrium!

☆ Thomas Bouchard

The Daffodils

I wandered lonely as a cloud
That floats on high o'er vales and hills,
When all at once I saw a crowd,
A host of golden daffodils,
Beside the lake, beneath the trees,
Fluttering and dancing in the breeze.

Continuous as the stars that shine
And twinkle on the milky way,
They stretch'd in never-ending line
Along the margin of a bay:
Ten thousand saw I at a glance
Tossing their heads in sprightly dance.

The waves beside them danced, but they
Out-did the sparkling waves in glee: —
A Poet could not but be gay
In such a jocund company!
I gazed — and gazed — but little thought
What wealth the show to me had brought;

For oft, when on my couch I lie
In vacant or in pensive mood,
They flash upon that inward eye
Which is the bliss of solitude;
And then my heart with pleasure fills,
And dances with the daffodils.

William Wordsworth

⮂ *Dance Is...* ⮂

...an art that imprints on the soul. It is with you every moment, even after you give it up. It is with you every moment of your day and night.

@   Shirley MacLaine

...called upon to express the loftiest emotions of the human soul.

@   André Levinson

...to bring into ideal balance the essentially instrumental, physical possibilities of your capricious, imperfect body with the possibilities of your soul, which is eternally renewing itself and constantly demanding new expression.

@   Natalia Makarova

...the product of the necessity for pure emotional expression.

@   La Meri

...a moment and then it is finished.

@   José Limón

...the pure act of metamorphosis.

◎ Paul Valéry

...more than technique, line, proportion, and balance. It is as if the performer and spectator come together to hold in their hands a bird with a broken wing. The creature can be felt to stir, to struggle for freedom. Its life responds to human warmth; its wing might brush your cheek as it flies away.

◎ Gelsey Kirkland

...to create, and in creating live
A being more intense, that we endow with form
Our fancy, gaining as we give
The life we image.

◎ George Gordon, Lord Byron

...an opening up, a submission to the dear, unwilled forces of human life.

◎ Agnes de Mille

❋ Dance as an Art ❋

Dance, and let the dreams of poets half-forgotten,
Speak through you as never spoke their printed pages;
Dance, and let the pictured visions of the painters
Move and speak and breathe and tear our quickened heartstrings;
Dance, and in the throbbing joy of rhythm and gesture,
Music, poetry, and painting melt together.

Joel Elias Springarn

The dance is not a lonely art. In its most complete manifestation it bears the proportion and balance of great temples; it dramatizes the emotions of mankind; it embodies the color and richness of great paintings; it makes live the beauty of line and form of statues; it charts the measures of poems; it traces the beautiful melodic patterns and visualizes the harmony of music.

Norma Gould

The most genuine of all art forms is the dance. Its artistic medium is the living human being and not merely one part of it but the whole... body from the soles of the feet to the top of the head. For anyone completely sensitive to art, music and poetry can only truly become comprehensible through the art of the dance.

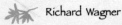 Richard Wagner

Dance is an ephemeral, a fleeting art. To describe this momentum, every movement on stage, in words is virtually impossible.

Mikhail Baryshnikov

I believe that dance is the oldest, noblest, and
    most cogent of the arts.
I believe that dance is the most perfect symbol of
    the activity of God and His angels.
I believe that dance has the power to heal, mentally
    and physically.
I believe that true education in the art of dance
    is education of the whole man.

Ted Shawn

The dance is an art wonderfully qualified to objectify the great, sustaining, inner rhythms of existence.

Jean Erdman

Dance as an art, when understood, is the province of every human being.

Margaret N. H'Doubler

Dance as Poetry

Dancing is silent poetry.

Simonides

The Gods have meant
That I should dance
And in some mystic hour
I shall move to unheard rhythms
Of the cosmic orchestra of heaven,
And you will know the language
Of my wordless poems
And will come to me,
For that is why I dance.

Ruth St. Denis

How graceful Maria leads the dance!
She's life itself. I never saw a foot
So nimble and so elegant; it speaks,
And the sweet whispering poetry it makes
Shames the musician.

Robert Burns

Dance is an acted poem, sparkling with images.

The Monthly Chronicle, 1838

Can a poem say my heart
While I stand apart?
I myself would be the song,
I myself would be the rhyme,
Moving delicately along;
And my steps would make the time,
And the stanzas be my rest.

What can I say with the words of my lips?
Oh, let me speak from my toes' tips
Of my treasure and my zest!

Dancing, I can tell every sweet —
Slow and soft, soft and fleet.
Dancing, I can tell every ill,
All my inmost wish fulfil,
All my sorrowing I can heal.
Oh, to reveal
With the bending of my head,
With the curving of my hand,
What no poem has ever said,
What no words could understand!
Things for a book too sad, too gay,
The verses of my feet would say;
Telling sorrow, telling delight
Into the very marrow of men's sight.

☆ Helen Hoyt

Poet to Dancer

Moving with you
I dare
leap up
the curving stair of space
to lay a lucid meaning
on the air
and trace
an arc of language,
as a heartbeat
loud and bare;

only in love beside
or hate
can ebb and flow of flesh
so plain articulate,
can breast and palm and thigh
dazzling as wing of hummingbird
out-cry.

O, could the word
so speak,
reply,
be heard!

Bernice Kavinoky

How much, indeed, can be expressed in words,
In speech we show this as in poetry;
But graceful movement, as we have beheld,
We dare not render in descriptive terms;
The sight itself gives us the sense of value,
The lovely dance must be its own sole herald.

Johann Wolfgang von Goethe

Things I can't say in words
run through my body as I dance....
Because we feel the power
of speaking another language:
the language of dance.

Eleanor Schick

It is the body, subject to the harmony of the
steps it is executing, which speaks. And it speaks
to the heart in as direct a language as does music.

Natalia Makarova

❋ The Music of the Body ❋

Your body's motion is like music,
Her stride, ecstatical and bright,
Moves to the rhythm of dumb music,
The unheard music of delight.

— John Hall Wheelock

You leap like living music through the air.

— Babette Deutsch

I think of
music as fuel, its
spectrum of
energy governed
by tempi, volume,
and heart.

— Twyla Tharp

Dancing can reveal all the mystery that music conceals.

— Charles Baudelaire

Earth and water air
and fire her body

beats the ground it
flows it floats it

seems to burn she
burns herself away

until there is no
body there at all

but only the pure
elements moving as

music moves moving
from her into us

James Laughlin

One Friday night
Mom pulled out
Learning to Dance Is Fun
with diagrams of feet
and a long-play record,
while Dad watched,
like a patient
awaiting
the dentist's whining drill.

Mom counted softly
onetwo
onetwothree
through
　　fox trot
　　　　samba
　　　　　　cha-cha-cha
as Dad danced —
feet on the wrong legs.

Yet,
the next afternoon
before the ball left the bat
Dad danced deep
into the hole at short,
lunged,
backhanded
in the middle of a bad hop —
the ball
at the edge of the webbing —
then
twirling,
falling away:
a perfect peg
to first.

Paul B. Janeczko

There is nothing so necessary for men as dancing.... Without dancing a man can do nothing.... All the ills of mankind, all the tragic misfortunes that fill the history books, the blunders of politicians, the miscarriages of great commanders, all this comes from lack of skill in dancing.... When a man has been guilty of a mistake, either in ordering his own affairs, or in directing those of the State, or in commanding an army, do we not always say: So and so has made a false step in this affair?... And can making a false step derive from anything but lack of skill in dancing?

☆ Jean Baptiste Molière

Every child has a right to know how to achieve control of his body in order that he may use it to the limit of his ability for the expression of his own reactions to life. Even if he can never carry his efforts far enough to realize dance in its highest forms, he may experience the sheer joy of the rhythmic sense of free, controlled, and expressive movement, and through this know an addition to life to which every human being is entitled.

☆ Margaret N. H'Doubler

A Life in Dance

Dancers work and live from the inside.... They drive themselves constantly, producing a glow that lights not only themselves, but audience after audience. They personify life itself.

They are elegant and strange-looking. Long and short, distinctive and nondescript; generous and selfish, one-tracked and no-tracked. But they know how to come alive like no other creature on earth and live to do so.

Murray Louis

Dancing appears glamorous, easy, delightful. But the path to the paradise of the achievement is not easier than any other. There is fatigue so great that the body cries, even in its sleep. There are times of complete frustration, there are daily small deaths. Then I need all the comfort that practice has stored in my memory, a tenacity of faith.

Martha Graham

The final and wished-for transparency of the body as an instrument and as a channel to the source of energy becomes possible under the discipline the dancer sets for himself — the rigid limitations he works within, in order to arrive at freedom.

Merce Cunningham

You have to be obsessed with dance to do dance; it's not something you play with. The commitment must be there, and the involvement total.

Alvin Ailey

Dancing is a way of life. From daily class to the heady pursuit of artistic perfection, dancers exist in a perpetual state of learning, reaching beyond personal limitations to realize their potential. A dancer's work, like a garden, is never completed but always growing. At its best, it transcends ordinary experience by expressing an essential part of our being through movement. We enter another realm filled with joy, exhilaration, and rapture.

Linda H. Hamilton, Ph.D.

Fine dancing, I believe, like virtue, must be its own reward.

Jane Austen

✩ ✩ The Magic of the Stage ✩ ✩

No thrill, physical or spiritual, could compare with those moments of power onstage — pity the person who is not a dancer!

✩ Sandra Noll Hammond

There have been certain moments on the stage when I suddenly had a feeling of completeness. Even disguised as a dancer, I felt like a total being. This has happened perhaps four or five times during my entire dancing career. It was a feeling of *I am*. At those moments, I had that indescribable sensation of being everywhere and nowhere. I had the sense of being universal.

✩ Erik Bruhn

It's a very, very delicate process being able onstage to peel open all those layers that you cover your heart with. But you do it, because there is a context — a flow — a beginning, middle, and end that you can trust. There is a sense of beauty that is retained, and a poetry that makes you survive.

✩ Peter Sparling

Being onstage... it's like a sacrifice — and I give myself completely. The moment I'm onstage, things become multiplied and magnified. It's like having an atomic reactor inside me. There is a chain reaction and, suddenly, my whole body bursts into flame.

☆ Rudolph Nureyev

Nothing so clearly and inevitably reveals the inner man than movement and gesture. It is quite possible, if one chooses, to conceal and dissimulate behind words or paintings or statues or other forms of human expression, but the moment you move you stand revealed, for good or ill, for what you are.

☆ Doris Humphrey

A true artist should have no secrets. On the stage, you must be able to transmit every emotion to the spectator.

☆ Anna Pavlova

❋ The Spirit of Dance ❋

God's in me when I dance.
God, making Spring
Out of his thoughts
And building worlds
By wishing.
God
Laughing at his own
Queer fancies,
Standing awed,
And sobbing;
Musing,
Dreaming,
Throbbing;
Commanding;
Creating —
God's in me
When I dance.

Mary Carolyn Davies

Dancers know that the mind, body, and spirit are inextricably intertwined.... The miraculous magic of expression overrides everything. It becomes everything.... You are dancing with God. You are dancing with yourself. You are dancing in the light.

Shirley MacLaine

Dance is bigger than the physical body.... When you extend your arm, it doesn't stop at the end of your fingers, because you're dancing bigger than that; you're dancing spirit.

Judith Jamison

She comes — the spirit of the dance!
And but for those large, eloquent eyes,
Where passion speaks in every glance,
She'd seem a wanderer from the skies.

Frances Sargeant Osgood

In a Dancer's Heart...

I couldn't live without dancing. If I had never had the opportunity to discover that I could dance — that I wanted to dance more than anything — I know I would have been a different person, and I believe that I would not have had the happiness that my life has given me.

Melissa Hayden

Let the music play,
I would dance alway —
Dance till the dawn of the bright young day!
Wild notes are sounding — swift lights are glancing,
And I — I am mad with the rapture of dancing —
Mad with a breathless delight.

Grace Denio Litchfield

To fling my arms wide
In some place of the sun,
To whirl and to dance
Till the white day is done.
Then rest at cool evening
Beneath a tall tree
While night comes on gently,
    Dark like me —
That is my dream!

Langston Hughes

It seemed to me as I stood on the hills that my whole life lay before me. The descending grassy slopes filled me with a passion to run, to roll in delirium, to wreck my body on the earth. Space means this to a dancer — or to a child! The descent through the air, the finding of earth-footage, the embracing and struggle with the fundamental ground. These are to a dancer what strong scents are to an animal.

Agnes de Mille

I am a dancer. When I pray
I do not gather thoughts with clumsy thread
Into poor phrases. Birds all have a way
Of singing home the truth that they are birds,
And so my loving litany is said
Without the aid of words.

Amanda Benjamin Hall

Those moments when my mind surrenders and my body takes over and moves of its own accord, governed only by muscles and reflexes — falling where it wants, stopping as it can, building the momentum to speed — are the only instances when I recognize true order. The body, outside the mind's control, moves intuitively.

Twyla Tharp

Dance Is for Everyone

There is a bit of insanity in dancing that
does everybody a great deal of good.

◎ Edwin Denby

It is people's movement that consoles us.
If the leaves of a tree did not move,
how sad would be the tree — and
so should we.

◎ Edgar Degas

I do still believe that when dancing is *right*, the
movement possesses a logic common to us all.

◎ Twyla Tharp

Every person's body is infused with the spirit of dance. It simply lives in each of us, waiting for us to exercise its powers of freedom and joy.

Gloria Duval

The dance... breaks the shackles... of the rigid human form and expresses for our benefit the things that we require to make us know wholeness.

Jean Erdman

We are all dancers. We use movement to express ourselves — our hungers, pains, angers, joys, confusions, fears — long before we use words, and we understand the meanings of movements long before we understand those of words. (Just as we understand the meaning of music, the music in the voice, long before we understand those of the voice's words.) And we continue to express ourselves with movement throughout the span of our lives.

Franklin Stevens

Why Dance?

Whenever there is sadness,
   you must dance away your tears.
Whenever there is loss,
   you must dance yourself to the moon.
Whenever a child is born,
   you must dance an unbroken circle.
Whenever you fall in love,
   you must dance together and find
   how dancing and contentment are the same.

☆ Nancy Wood

For this is my message, the message of a dancer.
Within your being, within your mind and your living body,
   lies a world of joy and power.
Within you lies a kingdom that you know little of.
The kingdom of fearless living, of sharing love, and the
   unfolding glory of your infinite being.
All this and more is yours.

☆ Ruth St. Denis

As long as man is responsive to the forces of life and the universe, there will be dance.

☆ Margaret N. H'Doubler

As the dance is born with man, it will exist as long as man exists. As it exists in life and nature everywhere in thousands of disguises, it will even survive man and stand at the cradle of what may come after him. Since nothing stands still but is in eternal flow whose rhythm is the universal pulsebeat of movement, the dance will be when the world will no longer be and another world will take its place.

☆ Walter Sorell

Dancing as an art, we may be sure, cannot die out, but will always be undergoing a rebirth. Not merely as an art, but also as a social custom, it perpetually emerges afresh from the soul of the people.

☆ Havelock Ellis

ACKNOWLEDGMENTS

We gratefully acknowledge the permission granted by the following authors, publishers, and authors' representatives to reprint poems or excerpts from their publications.

Alfred A. Knopf, Inc., a division of Random House, Inc. for "The world of dance..." from A DANCER'S WORLD by Margot Fonteyn. Copyright © 1979 Southern Maid Ltd. And for "...to bring into ideal" and "It is the body" from A DANCE AUTOBIOGRAPHY by Natalia Makarova. Copyright © 1979 by Natalia Makarova Karkar. And for "To fling my arms..." from "Dream Variations" from THE COLLECTED POEMS OF LANGSTON HUGHES by Langston Hughes. Copyright © 1994 by the Estate of Langston Hughes. And for "There is a bit..." from DANCE WRITINGS by Edwin Denby, edited by Robert Cornfield and William MacKay. Copyright © 1986 by Yvonne and Rudolph Burkhardt. All rights reserved.

Wesleyan University Press for "The dance is one of many..." from THE LANGUAGE OF DANCE by Mary Wigman, translated from the German by Walter Sorell. Copyright © 1966 by Walter Sorell.

Doubleday, a division of Random House, Inc. for "I feel that the essence...," "I think the reason...," and "Dancing appears glamorous..." from BLOOD MEMORY by Martha Graham. Copyright © 1991 by the Estate of Martha Graham. And for "...more than technique..." from DANCING ON MY GRAVE by Gelsey Kirkland with Greg Lawrence. Copyright © 1986 by Gelsey Kirkland. And for "I couldn't live..." from DANCER TO DANCER by Melissa Hayden. Copyright © 1981 by Melissa Hayden. All rights reserved.

Liveright Publishing Corporation for "How can I describe..." from MY LIFE by Isadora Duncan. Copyright © 1927 by Horace Liveright, Inc., renewed 1955 by Liveright Publishing Corp. All rights reserved.

New Directions Publishing Corporation for "To leap becomes..." from "Relearning the Alphabet" from POEMS 1968–1972 by Denise Levertov. Copyright © 1970 by Denise Levertov. All rights reserved.

The Los Angeles Times for "There's a reward..." by Robert Weiss from "Doctors Bow to Dancers' Special Need," LA Times, June 11, 1981 by William Trombley. Copyright © 1981 by the Los Angeles Times. All rights reserved.

Ommation Press for "When I leap..." from VICTIMS OF THE LATEST DANCE CRAZE by Cornelius Eady. Copyright © 1985 by Cornelius Eady. All rights reserved.

DanceMagazine and John Gruen for "I dance, because..." by Ghislaine Thesmar (DM, August 1979), "There have been..." by Erik Bruhn (DM, June 1986), "It's a very..." by Peter Sparling (DM, April 1987), and "Being onstage is..." by Rudolph Nureyev (DM, July 1986). Copyright © 1979, 1986, 1987 by DanceMagazine. All rights reserved.

PeaceWorks Publications for "With a motion...," "The gods have...," and "For this is...," by Ruth St. Denis from WISDOM COMES DANCING, edited by Kamae A Miller. Copyright © 1997 by PeaceWorks International Network for Dances of Universal Peace, P.O. Box 55994, Seattle, WA 98155.

Threshold Books for "Dance, when you're..." by Jalal Al-Din Rumi from THE ESSENTIAL RUMI, translated by Coleman Barks. Copyright © 1995 by Coleman Barks. All rights reserved.

Princeton Book Company Publishers and John Gruen for "The esthetics of dance..." by Arthur Mitchell from PEOPLE WHO DANCE. Copyright © 1988 by John Gruen.

Larry D. Tyler for "Our love is like...." Copyright © 2001 by Larry D. Tyler. All rights reserved.

Donald I. Fine, an imprint of Penguin Putnam, Inc., for "Human beings are born..." from NOTHING TO HIDE by Robert La Fosse and Andrew Mark Wentink. Copyright © 1987 by Robert La Fosse and Andrew Mark Wentink.

Charles Portolano for "Born to Dance." Copyright © 2001 by Charles Portolano. All rights reserved.

Nancy Wood for "Why Dance?" and "All My Life is a Dance" from MANY WINTERS, published by Doubleday, a division of Random House, Inc. Copyright © 1974 by Nancy Wood. All rights reserved.

Dr. Dorothy Buck for "The call to dance..." from THE DANCE OF LIFE by Dorothy Buck, published by Paragon House. Copyright © 1987 by Dorothy Buck. All rights reserved.

Diane Mariechild for "The dancer moves..." from THE INNER DANCE by Diane Mariechild with Shuli Goodman. Copyright © 1987 by Diane Mariechild. All rights reserved.

Columbia University Press for "Movement is the essence..." from THE DANCER'S IMAGE by Walter Sorell. Copyright © 1971 by Columbia University Press. All rights reserved. And for "Suddenly I see..." by Thomas Bouchard, "...the product of..." by La Meri, "The dance is an art..." and "The dance...breaks the shackles..." by Jean Erdman, "The final and wished-for..." by Merce Cunningham, and "All the dance is born..." by Walter Sorell from DANCE HAS MANY FACES. Copyright © 1951 by Walter Sorell.

William Morrow, a division of HarperCollins Publishers, for "Dancing is like..." from SAVION! MY LIFE IN TAP by Savion Glover and Bruce Weber. Copyright © 1999 by Savion Glover. All rights reserved.

Paul Plotz and the Estate of Helen Plotz for "The rhythms of..." from UNTUNE THE SKY, compiled by Helen Plotz. Copyright © 1957 by Thomas Y. Crowell Publishing Company.

Bantam Books, an imprint of Random House, Inc. for "...an art that imprints..." and "Dancers know that..." from DANCING IN THE LIGHT by Shirley MacLaine. Copyright © 1985 by Shirley MacLaine. All rights reserved.

Princeton Book Company, publisher of Dance Horizon Books, for "Dance is a moment..." by José Limón from DANCE IS A MOMENT by Barbara Pollack and Charles Humphrey Woodford. Copyright © 1995 by Barbara Pollack and Charles Humphrey Woodford. All rights reserved.

Harold Ober Associates Ltd. For "...an opening up..." and "It seemed to me..." from DANCE TO THE PIPER by Agnes de Mille. Copyright © 1951, 1952 by Agnes de Mille. All rights reserved.

Jacob's Pillow Dance Festival for "I believe that..." from "Credo" by Ted Shawn. Copyright © 1970 by Jacob's Pillow Dance Festival. All rights reserved.

The University of Wisconsin Press for "Dance as an art...," "As long as man...," and "Every child has..." from DANCE: A CREATIVE ART EXPERIENCE by Margaret N. H'Doubler. Copyright © 1957 by the Regents of the University of Wisconsin. Copyright renewed 1985 by the University of Wisconsin Foundation. All rights reserved.

The Virginia Quarterly Review for "Poet to Dancer" by Bernice Kavinoky. Copyright © 1956 by The Virginia Quarterly Review.

Simon and Schuster Books for Young Readers, an imprint of Simon and Schuster Children's Publishing Division, for "Things I can't say..." from I HAVE ANOTHER LANGUAGE: THE LANGUAGE IS DANCE by Eleanor Schick. Copyright © 1992 by Eleanor Schick. All rights reserved.

The Joy Harris Literary Agency, Inc. for "I think of music...," "Those moments when...," and "I do still believe..." from PUSH COMES TO SHOVE by Twyla Tharp, published by Bantam Books, a division of Random House, Inc. Copyright © 1992 by Twyla Tharp. All rights reserved.

Moyer Bell for "Earth and water..." from "Martha Graham" from THE COLLECTED POEMS OF JAMES LAUGHLIN. Copyright © 1957, 1994 by James Laughlin. All rights reserved.

Orchard Books, an imprint of Scholastic, Inc., for "One Friday night..." from "Mystery" from BRICKYARD SUMMER by Paul B. Janeczko. Copyright © 1989 by Paul B. Janeczko. All rights reserved.

St. Martin's Press, LLC, for "Dancers work and live..." from INSIDE DANCE ESSAYS by Murray Louis. Copyright © 1980 by Murray Louis. All rights reserved.

Birch Lane Press, an imprint of Kensington Publishing Corporation, for "You have to be..." from REVELATIONS by Alvin Ailey with A. Peter Bailey. Copyright © 1995 by Alvin Ailey and A. Peter Bailey. All rights reserved.

Mayfield Publishing Company for "No thrill..." from BALLET BASICS by Sandra Noll Hammond. Copyright © 1993, 1984, 1974 by Mayfield Publishing Company. All rights reserved.

Charles Humphrey Woodford for "Nothing so clearly..." by Doris Humphrey, found in THE DANCE HAS MANY FACES, edited by Walter Sorell, published by The World Publishing Company. Copyright © 1951 by Walter Sorell.

Cowan, DeBaets, Abrahams, and Shepherd for "Dance is bigger..." from DANCING SPIRIT by Judith Jamison with Howard Kaplan. Copyright © 1993 by Judith Jamison. All rights reserved.

Avon Books, an imprint of HarperCollins Publishers, for "We are all dancers..." from DANCE AS LIFE by Franklin Stevens. Copyright © 1976 by Franklin Stevens. All rights reserved.

A careful effort has been made to trace the ownership of selections used in this anthology in order to obtain permission to reprint copyrighted materials and give proper credit to the copyright owners. If any error or omission has occurred, it is completely inadvertent, and we would like to make corrections in future editions provided that written notification is made to the publisher:

SPS STUDIOS, INC., P.O. Box 4549, Boulder, Colorado 80306.